STEPPING ON THE CRACKS

**North Northumberland Libraries
Limerick & Poetry Competition
2007
Patron Saints of Britain**

1st Prize Limerick Section

NORTHUMBERLAND
COUNTY COUNCIL

For James

STEPPING ON THE CRACKS

Amanda White

FLAMBARD

ACKNOWLEDGEMENTS

Some poems in this collection have previously appeared in:
Ambit, Envoi, The Interpreter's House, Magma, Mslexia,
Poetry Life, Rialto, The Source and *Staple.*

'The Stay', 'Rests in the Music', 'The Giraffe House' and 'Granny's
Blue Poodle Period' were published in the anthology *The Nerve:*
The 1998 Book of Writing Women (Virago). 'The Giraffe House' also
appeared in a *TLS/Poems on the Underground* pamphlet in 1996.
'Singular' and 'Disaster Movie (Closing Credits)' were runners-up in the
single poem category of The New Writer Poetry Prizes 1998 and published
in a paperback volume of winners, *The Piano on Fire*, in May 1999.
'Legal' won second prize in the Artistic Licence Open Poetry
Competition 1997 and was published on the internet. 'Granny's
Blue Poodle Period' won second prize in the 11th Poetry Life
Competition 1997. 'His Parents' appeared on number 38 and 73
London buses in 1995/96 for Big Words; it was also a runner-up in the
Capricorn International Poetry and Short Story Competition 1998
and published in a winners' anthology. 'Dusting for Fingerprints'
appeared in the Swanage Arts Festival Competition 1997 anthology.

The photographs used for the cover are by Julian Brown,
except for that of the author by Andrew Gillman.

Flambard Press wishes to thank Northern Arts for its financial support.

First published in England in 1999 by Flambard Press
Stable Cottage, East Fourstones, Hexham NE47 5DX

Typeset by Harry Novak
Cover design by Gainford Design Associates
Printed by Cromwell Press, Trowbridge, Wiltshire

A CIP catalogue record for this book
is available from the British Library.

ISBN 1 873226 35 7

CONTENTS

I: The Apple Never Falls Far from the Tree

II: Fine Words Butter No Parsnips

I

The Apple Never Falls
Far from the Tree

WISHBONES

In the beginning was the body proverb, polite sounds and
family sentences from the infrangible Logos of granny's lips
forming the pattern of her mother before her, and back
further to a second sight that saw fear in the countenance of a
babe screaming danger, crossed cutlery on a plate. A neck of
old rocks kept landlocked tales from the Yorkshire dales of
her youth to the married life of avenues down south in a
chalet bungalow that warded off elves and other neighbours
with thick nets and a red herring of crazy paving in the back.

Fighting over the wishbones of endless Sunday roasts lives
depended on the winning break of cartilage, a dull snap
rocking up a Noah of consequences in a dining room that
took the shape of good and bad luck, more Delphi than
Eastbourne. More oracle than granny, all eyes sat upon
the near-broken mirror of her sage old face that had
seldom rolled but gathered moss-green eyes, waiting,
from a stitch-in-time orange mouth held in a wise line,
for sayings to inoculate the child from a diphtheria of
loose talk, to make the hieroglyphic of my spine,
too young to translate, sit up straight to chain the mind,
to speak only when spoken to when she saw me straining
to break out and walk beneath the ladder of her gaze,
or when she wasn't looking (even with third-eye moles)
take a chance and hide Brussels sprouts up my sleeve.

Granny made me a new name, called me Goig, as if born
from a once-upon-a-time dragon not a mother who knew
how to make a good Victoria sandwich. She magicked up the
sound so it felt like being the only ones who knew how to do
a card trick. When I held her hand on the way to the Mace
shop and she called me Goig at the end of every sentence, it
seemed to stop me getting run over or bruising my knees.

While passing the sugar she passed on those strange secrets,
on the first of the month a grace of rabbits for good luck,
before murdering the pale flesh of a grapefruit that often spat
back a tart dagger to her eye, a last stand that brought a silent
curse to pursed lips and a discreet, lightning dab of hanky
(ironed and folded), returned to an invisible drawer in her
hip before carrying on regardless, leaving me deciphering
the ritual, perhaps something she would warn me about
when older, a sign of deformed babies or bad husbands.

Meals amened with chat about the forecast, rain threatening
to break the artex, make us forget that umbrellas can be evil
when without thinking I might leave one drying indoors,
as I did the other day with grown-up hands and worries,
hoping that below the ground she was dry and comfy as
granny would want to be, a sensible mac of warm earth about
her, in the end a change proving in death as good as a rest.

INSIDE THE HOLLOW ROCK

'When hollow rocks retain the sound of blustering
Winds, which all night long had rous'd the fear.'
         (John Milton, *Paradise Lost*)

Phone calls come in isobars of bad weather
I sleep inside the hollow rock
find muscles in the guttering below my ribs

   The anaesthetist wakes me

I live on a jugular avenue of trees fed up with the view
avoid cars and outstretched hands
feel sick all the time and tell my friends 'I'm fine'

   Shadows of pretend angels wrap me in swaddling blankets
   Beneath my body a plastic cover comforts me still

Tis night and I listen for the magic of my own breathing
a shudder of water into a glass and something soluble
then five paces back to bed and the south pole of ever dark skies

   You bring me a 250mg ponstan capsule
   you bring me golden tea and ham sandwiches
   you show me the blood between my legs

Tracer sirens down on the hard tarmac
someone is lying disused in casualty antiseptically wiped clean
and I take my head back into the indifference of a pillow

   Beside me a woman sterilised and her baby aborted – weeps
   I reach towards her and try to soak up the hurt – faint
   and in my womb the leftovers come to life
   nematode worms reaching for daylight

Time for shedding skin and undressing
behind my wall a neighbour considers suicide
and I can say I saw you once in the street and passed on

> *Inside the belly of a cab at high noon*
> *arriving at the unsuspecting threshold of a house like any other*
> *the receptionist logs in each appointment running to time*
> *you call my name, I pay my money and you smile*
> *wide cunt smile 'No' you say 'I never had one myself'*

I prize open a blackhead from my shoulder
brush the bed free of crumbs
reorder the unwelcome snarl of creases in old sheets

> *Behind these suburban bay windows*
> *knickerless women tread their way to the theatre*
> *once inhabited by easy chairs and coffee tables*
> *and now it's my turn to climb the scaffold steps*
> *and I roll a sleeve while the doctor tells me*
> *'You have a nice vein'*

It is that sleeping time again
the count to ten but never quite making it
trapped inside this mingled state of transient being.

FOREPLAY

Pillow man was a soft and happy place
that made me feel something tingly
when I wrapped tiny legs around him,
playing a new game, pressing and rolling,
not really knowing why, but keeping
him secret and dragging him out from
the dark covers if mummy came to check
on me, of course then making out he
was just a pillow under my head
and sleeping, not touching me down there.

Pebble man was not one but many
mouths on shingle beaches in summer,
when I lay down on my stomach
and found that better than sun-bathing
I could kiss you all, shamelessly,
without preferring one above another,
just something to practise on, and afterwards
all you might see was a young girl
throwing away a stone, never thinking
she had learnt the art of using.

Book man lived in the dirty passages
of my grandfather's paperbacks next
to the coupons he raped from newspapers,
he was a real man who looked just like
Richard Gere and knew what to do and say
at the same time, not like the first boy man,
no better than stones, who bit me when
he kissed me and tried after clumsy
tongues to be a pillow and go down there,
making me close my eyes and pretend.

EXPLORER

'"Who are you?" said the Caterpillar.'
        (Lewis Carroll, *Alice's Adventures in Wonderland*)

This is the unmapped distance of a gaze
from skerry eye to spiracle mouth,
where a Sisyphean finger
makes uphill tracings to roll
back the trick of the familiar.

Unpeeled skin reflects a swift erosion,
the photograph in which I say
no likeness can be found, not knowing if this face
makes up any one solid constellation or fits
the name that turns the head to face others.

Eyebrows curious and vast
speak a sentence which cannot translate,
lips sink and curve with eternal meanderings
and a pool of dry depths and brief fossils
rests in the merest fleck of a cheek's continent.

The desert of my own face
remains an untravelled and sterile place,
reveals only surface cracks and
tracks of laughter and worry
that have marked but not conquered me.

Attracted by firm lines, I prepare,
an easy circumnavigation of a mouth in blood,
step into the unmirrored street and
retreat into a landmark of mapped out features
seemingly unworthy of second glances.

ACQUIRING THE TASTE

I met my father perhaps as many times as I have fingers
usually at meal times in that smooth creamy county of Berkshire
safe distances and table manners
eating somehow easier than talking
uncomfortable cheek kisses wiped clean by obligatory serviettes.

I turned up on him at just eighteen all sickly, sweet and tempting
and he drank me in with a double G&T and kept back the tears
it was a quick and painful aperitif
he sat like a fat and over-ripe plum
hardly that slim and dashing figure from the sixties seen in a photograph.

The courses that followed were well ordered but far too rich
thick and strong wines relaxing you into the telling of dirty jokes
I hung like the leftovers on your plate
a strange and untouched no-more child
drowning in luxurious restaurants and parting with stains on my dress.

When the coffee arrived you often spoke of that other family
those half-empty untried sisters and brothers I had and could not meet
the ones you shared most meals with
unlike our secret indulgences
you picking at me like a man just circulating at a cocktail party.

For one dinner only and after twenty years the three of us sat together
my father all meat and my mother a not-yet-dead still slippery fish
while I sat attempting to accompany
all vegetable and gravy
an awkward and well-reduced sauce of a once-secret love affair.

I imagined the dinners my mother and father must have had together
my conception from the thin belly of a well-buttered asparagus
exhausted aphrodisiacs and reservations
my mother's glass left unfilled
as you rushed home to stomach a cold supper with your wife.

We rarely delved into the à-la-carte staying within the ease of set menus
you swallowing me whole while I spat out the pips from you
making deliberate cuts and slicings
your eyes oystering down my throat
tasting something more than the healthy father/daughter relationship.

I wanted to impress you and you tried to make up for lost time
but we never risked staying long enough for the food to go bad
fearing sell-by dates and packaging
and when at last I had decided to be greedy
you went and died leaving me with cravings and a bad aftertaste.

PRESSED FLOWERS

We lie, flattened by the weight of dreams and ourselves. Cartoon
splats, that is how we might laugh it all off. Some nights, tucked
in tighty tight, blackheads, so tempting to pick at, the ooze of

secrets disgusting and/or delicious straining to weep out and
linger in the here-and-now of half-light while the all-seeing blinds
make a shadow play between the lines of what we might

or… tighter still there in our chests: the near miss on the M25,
Romanian orphans on the news, the miscarried baby we flushed
away, the hit he called a slap – hinged worries bunnying about

for attention, each one straining to get out from under the stamp
collections, old photograph albums and other lost trails. The
heartbeat screws right down to a dead-headed stop, a clear

memory surfaces, bobbing up through the rippled distractions; the
way the daisies danced, fluttering albino lashes, they seemed to
match our mood, young love, keen, shimmer shake of hands

near touching, late summer sun drinking us down as we picked
the one out from the rest and snapped it shut between the
pages of Agatha's *Death on the Nile* or was it more literary,

Joyce's *Portrait*? And there the heat haze flickers and lets go to an
uncertain twilight and whatever, the book and its contents are lost
or borrowed or hoping to be found, it seemed important

at the time. That same daisy, slow strangled, cruel to be kind,
remains withered yet strangely evocative, more wheeze than
flutter these days, but struggling all the same to be more than

nothing: the letters you save in an old *Black Magic* box, that
snatched kiss from a stranger on the Central line, the yelpcry of
our first born. Its petals curl in upon itself, the dry ghost of a

lost scent, some mummified sample of 'Obsession', shut up in an old *Vogue* languishing down the doctors, near rubbish, cover well fingered, left for dead. By morning we throw off the covers

again and emerge time-travelled but none the wiser, slipping easily into form and underwear. We blow down the road, unpicked, resembling others, perhaps pink-tipped carnations

bought in a hurry from the garage. Poised on the curb, we seem ready to disperse but pull together at the last moment, fix our place to cross the road, take each other's hand without thinking.

TURNING CIRCLE

Topped and tailed
the last four coaches neck their way on to Hastings,
deposit me at the end of the line where I once began.
I feel ill in the same way as you don't feel ill after a hot bath.
The town centre takes me back with a welcome of overweight
Hoppa buses bumping and grinding a clumsy conga, proof of life
on other planets and Eastbourne.

To the west of everywhere
a compass sea still churns it all over, sicking up thick
grey gobs of surf onto shingle dreaming of better days
edging out from a patio. The lifers listen to war medleys at the
bandstand, deck chairs arranged in a half-circle, while the
rest of the statistics stay, ever sheltering in the Arndale,
discount and peeling.

Ghosts of myself pass by,
shopping for cheap earrings, buying 'Dancing Queen' from Max's
Records by the station (now a Car Phone Warehouse), getting
pissed on cider down Seaside on a too-small swing swinging,
watching Roy and Dina snogging on the roundabout. I reach for
an imaginary gun, check in a panic, there, the return ticket safe
inside the holster of my wallet.

I go to a pub where I once
went regularly. The name has changed, the wallpaper too but
the faces seem the same, careful slices of lemon, flat on their
backs on a saucer at the bar. I order a red wine, a mistake, size up
the contents of evenings, torpid words and nervous teenage
conversation, who fancied who, telling ourselves we knew it all
and were having a great time.

There is a man on his own at the bar
(there is always a man on his own at the bar), 'Odd' the eyes seem
to say safe in pints and crowds. There is a woman alone by the stairs,
'Tart' the lips move to say, so I have just the one drink and leave,
dissolve back into streets wintering out the last of the Wallace Arnolds.
I slip down to the prom where the crazy golf locked-up and in
need of attention never looked so sane.

The pier, half-land, half-sea, is open,
ten-minute speedboat rides at the end by Dixieland Disco
(first tongue kiss), glass animals pleading to escape and a girl I went
to school with is giving out change in the amusement arcade.
She had big tits when she was ten, we were jealous then,
now the same highlights in her hair are lifeless and the popularity
and cool of smoking JPS distant,

'Ten tens.' We do not exchange addresses.

MOTHER'S HOMEMADE MARMALADE

I need to get you
stuck between my teeth again

I don't want to murder you now
just cook away afternoons swapping recipes

DISASTER MOVIE (CLOSING CREDITS)

Your angry kiss remains the last sense
I have of my own body,
the rescue team will find it,
a fallen crab apple
rotting in a foreign garden
discarded for real evidence
and recognisable personal effects.

You come to identify my left ear
preserved by snow in the Alps
a snarl of turbine piercing the lobe.
And you can't be sure.
Did you ever pay attention to detail?
But you keep me in your freezer
in case you need someone to listen.

DAYS OUT

When the tides begin to confuse you, better to stay
still, tethered to the granite of a recovered armchair,
comfy safe daytime. This is when the roomscape

tricks you again into thinking it can be bigger than
it is, bringing the weather inside past the old socks
guarding the draft, playing anaconda, while you shore

up the afternoons with keepsakes and the remains
of films dotting the horizon. Here strangers and famous
people hold waists and conga along the curtain rail,

high up, mixing time with your time, that photograph
with Dolly on the Clifton suspension bridge, eyes
nearly shut, background a little out of focus. Occasional

visitors bring toffees, poisoned perhaps, but you eat them
anyway, swallow a silent conquest and laugh at the wrong
moments as they shed their skin and dirty gossip on

your upholstery. Sometimes you decide to tell them
a little about the past, lives that drew you to this
solid place and an emergency bell; you see as you

tell, as if for the first time, a flicker of understanding,
a ghost of yourself disappearing down the throat of
piers and beyond, picnics endured more than marches

through Italy, that nice chap that comes to chat when
you doze off, the prisoner of war you took to the cinema
in Rome. The visitors deal smiles accordingly, so near yet…

Nazis… and cyclists and people who let their dogs foul
the promenade. Michael Fish seems one to trust, loose talk
drizzle, neighbourly. The dark comes earlier, creeping up

from the kitchenette where indecisions and bad memories have been divided by sensible cutlery that could still cut a wrist if you wanted but butter crackers before bed instead.

THE ENDANGERED SPECIES OF UNCLE

The lounge had been redecorated
like the growth of cousins
unearthed after three years
and I feel younger as my Uncle bends to kiss me
almost fifty.

There is a confusion
in nieces and nephews embalmed in warm kitchens of
flat-tongued luncheons
and spineless relations who remember
birthdays more than the anonymous pedestrian you
choose not to run down.

Closets, cubicles,
the ageing house looks well,
photographs in their frames
counterfeiting a grin, familiar, strained.
We are all sitting down watching television
strung together with vague blood ties
and my Uncle has just pinched my bum.

Closets, cubicles,
the counting of guests at weddings and funerals
we guess it must be autumn
and time for death and marriage.
You look at me with eyes that saw me climb
plum trees at the age of twelve,
scrape my knee at three
and kiss your son at sixteen.
More of a tart than a niece
now politely you kiss me on the cheek.

I am see-through
sitting by the reproduction Victorian fireplace,
stroking your dogs as you watch the rugby and
shout at the fine footwork, the dodge, the try.
You have ten eyes and twenty fingers
undressing my privacy with relativity and a gift.
Uncles are just men with a privilege
and a well-concealed tongue kiss.

HUMAN

I have internal space, mind, body and room
to make improvement
slow-worming a view into the rain slash of windows.

I can make that leap from high rise
to concrete playground
and risk the splatter of colour mistaken for paint.

I have spirit to self-combust and turn veins to wicks
make fire rubbing breaths
to blow myself out and hope for fossils.

I can function, shop and count with four fingers at one time
follow form with careful footsteps
taking that route from the brain to the bathroom daily.

I can dream and remember being a child beneath parents
a glimpse of embryo
simmering in some belly called mother.

I can dive to the borders and explore less explored jungles
coming back with research
to add to information to make mountains, again.

I can look, listen and learn but with cunning
not really trying but giving
the appearance of being all there at one time.

I am more than dust so you all tell me
perhaps that is why
I remember my dreams and take buses.

ANKH

Ankh, the crux ansata, symbolised to Ancient Egyptians the life
to come with its three attributes: peace, happiness and serenity.

I am bench
cheap wood and poor vision
human and nettle natures fingering my plank limbs.

Knot eyes try to focus
on the Thames sludging through Richmond
where we used to walk the dogs and each other.

Dull draughts scoot through my slats
a poor chance at aeolian tunes
lost on a million lucky voices travelling the winds.

Dogs mess at my four feet
as if life wasn't hard enough
loving husband breaking my back in all weathers.

He leaves crumbs and bottom smells
to join those cruel hearts
carved into blossomless bones of everlasting arthritis.

Mocked by the sometime tickle of a butterfly
I am sure it is his mother
roving the world with a body of light wings.

I should have told him I preferred Lake Como
better still made sure you died before me
laid you to rest with 'in memory' lumbago.

SKIMMING STONES

A voodoo woman in the mountains
of the Sierra Maestra in Cuba,
keeps a rock in a glass of water
she calls Mother Earth
and from it magic speaks
the past, present and future.

You would not pick her out from a crowd
she just rolls around,
mongrel colouring,
seasoned by sale windows
down Oxford Street
riding on fashioned tides,
hole in her belly button
an arctic of interest, briefly,

moving with the moving
she no-thinking,
tarn-wet eyes sometime-sparkle
in the strobe light
of a late nightclub,
when others around
make her seem
more amethyst and appealing,

earlymorninglatenights
dried and dulled on strange beaches,
zones 3 and 4 and other coastal districts,
she washes home, unexceptional,
sleeps tight-curled, stone attracting stone
thrown sea-deep by weak arms
a one-bounce skim into the backswash
of cold, flat, tideless seas,

she waits for fossils and a fortunate wave
to lick her damp again,
she hopes to glister for a few hours
in the hot surf,
dreaming of tropical beaches
and bumps planed to sand,
falling weightless
from a shell-picking hand.

As we twist round three times
and she whips the sage leaves
Mother Earth tells her
I nearly died when I was twenty
and I wonder when I am stone
if I will see so clearly.

SWIFT TO ITS CLOSE

The title and last line are taken from the second
verse of 'Abide With Me' by H.F. Lyte.

She sits at a table for two
close to the wall
hums 'Abide With Me.'

She still has her teeth
and other pearls
around her neck of ravines.

Her dress is a medley of blues
those old tunes
and afternoon films.

She asks me 'Is it still cold out?'
weathers politely as I nod/smile
in the way people do at the old.

She has a new cardi
and agate-slice eyes
she says 'The clock is slow.'

She takes out five pounds
folds it into a card
writes 'Buy something nice.'

She is past that age
when you imagine
the body lying beneath.

She cries in private
waiting for Christmas cards
and news to arrive.

She eats fruit cake
leaves crumbs of worry
and other dead friends.

She asks 'Has it started raining?'
still hoping for conversation
turning back from the door.

She joins the street slowly
the drizzle washes her home
ebbs out life's little day.

STILLS

'Time is a blind guide.'
        (Anne Michaels, *Fugitive Pieces*)

Not yet born I cannot tell you where I was
or what I was doing when JFK got shot,
but when Uncle Harold died, pull focus,
eczema on the end of my right hand-middle finger
itching, and the place Mansfield Hospice
all cosy bungalow and too many magazines,
flowers standing in well-used vases lasting out the patients,
vulgar blooming
my own raw red roses showing up the yellowed melt of skin,

          you tell your story with glittering eye,
          the froufrou details crisper than personal moments
          important to have been in the right country
          a few states over but nudging up a proximity,
          as if you really heard the bullet shatter
          every woman making out like Jackie,

a smoked glass mug of tea going cold, flecks of brown
shavings separating off, by a trinity of get well cards,
the smell of pine air freshener mixed with dettol,
a man in the next bed doing the *Daily Express* crossword,
his wife trying to keep her hips and false teeth from slipping,
nervous smile as she does herself and her mac up to leave,
skate slide of cheap shoes over linoleum channels,
then silence as she hits home to carpet tiles,
small histories.
Uncle Harold puffing out a volcano,
reduced to a few words gulped down inside a life's tired continent,
the worry of a pyjama button struggling on the gibbet of a loose thread,
hanging,

a Vegas diner half-griddled
you follow the crush,
this was something worth leaving a breakfast to go cold,
you remember so well the dead pan of the street
ticker tape letters spangling the news above,
the whole world waiting, and you
not knowing whether he was dead or alive,

Velvet green eyes deep set inside his skull
transcend the deceit of a body
so I can recognise him again,
plumped out and living in the house where he was born,
Trent Street, Retford,
never married but surrounded by technology,
quietly inventing,

    I tell you I might have seen the movie,
    perhaps cheap-price Mondays Tottenham Court Road,
    but you are sure of your own technicolor,
    an instance more history than personal tragedy,
    a point we can all trace from and to
    your feelings enough to shake a century,
    millions like you still remembering,

my left hand holds on tight and stays warm as a once spent match,
a one-shot echo of his last breath,
screaming out Richard and Judy,
and I want this to matter enough
for the rest of the world to pebble-ring from his quiet heart stop,
as his hand slips from mine onto still clean sheets,

    you smile at the punchline, then tell me
    a newspaper man stood on the other side of the street,
    he wouldn't be selling any more papers that day,
    he wouldn't be selling any more papers that day,
    and more than saying you knew him you really miss him

as you say you miss your first husband
who died before his time, unspectacular,
heart attack, you have few details,
and if deaths are jealous of one another
I'd say he must be fuming.

behind him through the window to the car park,
the immaculate light of *B&Q* scuffs out the distance of drizzle-mist,
my first tear falls from a great height,
lid to chin,
its clear wet hope pausing weighty,
before throwing itself off into the dry fibres of a jumper
and evaporating as I walk away slow-mo,
knowing Uncle Harold will not shake a headline
but stutter through obituaries beside the classifieds,
an unfamous memory of a man who died from cancer at 72
and could no longer feel his fingers
to count on those who really knew him.

II

Fine Words Butter No Parsnips

GRANNY'S BLUE POODLE PERIOD

I thought of Picasso
at her bedside or
taking a walk into the lounge
where faces hung in still-life lines
gone quietly wonky in front of the
giant-size telly
spewing out daytime obscenities
a view on the real world
they had all left behind
accelerating fast on wheelchairs
pooing in their pants
down the icy floors
through the floppy
old vagina flaps of doors
into the geriatric ward.

Granny had Parkinson's
sat in her pink-blanket bed
insulting Albert her husband
swearing he was a homosexual
sure the Brazilian ancillary was
doing experiments with her wee
and I tried to retrieve some memory
that clear sight
before it got so bad
my little hand in hers
striding by the sea
her pointing out white horses
and the cross-channel ferry
instead of blue poodles
curled around her swollen feet.

We took it in shifts to visit and sit
with flowers by the living graveside
and on good days she sat up
looked out with her bright blue eyes
and made a stab at recognition
before collapsing into that
jigsaw of unmatching pieces
strangers by her bed
pretending to be relatives
our features in the wrong place
and once I imagined
I saw those blue poodles
even heard their barking
and they were smiling up at me
and wagging their tails.

THE GIRAFFE HOUSE

Untroubled by good or bad reviews
the giraffes sleep much of the time
when they're not snacking or just
hanging about on awkward corners.
They don't mind staying in, blinking
out at nothing in particular, that
other life they have only heard about,
passing by, there below, somehow hard
to focus on from such a height – not
unlike their neighbours of the short,
unpatterned and human kind, who
also live in captivity and zone one.

OUR LADY OF THE UMBRELLA

For a woman who lived on the streets in Holborn
and doesn't seem to live there anymore.

Uncelebrated angel crouching in pavement and doorway
under the same old, time-old umbrella of bent spokes,
caress of street, sweet Jesus
accommodating all weather,
ubiquitous shadow,
not playing house but living beneath hem lines,
holding out the altar of a hand.

Passers-by calculate with forgive-us eyes,
not wanting to look but noticing,
stopped by a chesty cough,
enough seismic to shake an empty highrise
gloating over all that warm space,
while beneath repossessed skies
her body scaffolds.

It's a miracle she's still alive,
humble bones resurrected daily
on unmarked gravestones,
and when it rains
there is no need to take shelter,
she just watches the upright souls
join her in a hallelujah of respectful umbrellas.

HIS PARENTS

They come up on the dry train early in the morning
his parents all steam and oil
greetings spread with fertiliser
about our house, which is their house
and talk to their son, who is my boyfriend,

and we have hoovered the carpet
polished the mirrors for that perfect double image
(And then he grew up and flew away)
and she asks him why we have bought a new fridge
when the old one would have done,

worried by the shortness of my skirt
the father sits defrosting
on the awkward bed settee
that we bought with the money they gave us
though rather for him than for me,

it is hard to remove all the dust
(And then he grew up and she took him from me)
I offer tea in odd mugs
the politeness is killing
a suggestion is made to go out,

they take us for al fresco pasta
she cuts up her spaghetti
and thinks as she watches the coil of my spoon
it is easier to use a knife
slyly checking her son to ensure three against one.

LIFE DRAWING

The fires and the heaters are all from the fifties
but your flesh undated
still
hangs over a chair
rare back bone
eyes following pencil lines

Women divorced they have come here to paint her
men in depression have come to be saved here
and she is silent
therapy
limp
replaced in the morning by a sheep's skull

She is iron
something hidden in her belly
and I saw her at a bus stop
dark scribbles of shadow
moving
and I was ashamed

Measuring against a finger
from here enough to hide you completely
and then the fresh angle down to the thigh
matt of pubic hair
a clumsy tracing on sugar paper
distracted

She has eyes beyond our counting
no arm but the arm of a statue
no sex but the spell of her name
and in her hair a straightness
defying the curl of our scratchings
the careful joining of limb to limb
each one of us wanting to move you

THE STAY

In your house not my house but welcoming
in my room once your room, spare and shifting
strange time now clocking a rip of afternoon
you downstairs preparing the carrots for death
and you had said stay as long as you like
but I saw the hard-cash balance of friendship
crack between the harsh laughter lines of your eyes
that pleasant offer to bring my friends over any time
and yet my stealing footsteps as I go to the toilet at night
having rehearsed every creak of landing
and held sheets around me for sound proofing
now I find myself announced into each room
eyed up suspiciously by possessions
fearful of inanimate objects going missing
that most precious of ornaments suddenly breaking
and the excuse of your words making light of accidents
as you frisk me for insurance policies.

I make friends with your bathroom and unfamiliar
brands of cosmetics, rape a blusher without touching
lock the door on this room for my leasing
with a mirror to guide fresh sight on features
and a place to hang my towel cousined close to yours
I take stock of belongings in new corners
the wait for where to make mess but not quite sure
the folded remnants of my life still born in boxes
with a view to the garden where idle birds whimper
getting used to the way the sash falls if opened
and the change in the temperature with each
flick of heating knowing when to switch on
and off again the hot water guilty of over-indulgence
while I steal a drop of bubble bath and listen
to your movements in the kitchen beneath me
waiting for a sudden noise to give away my bearings
as you shout upstairs I am welcome to join you for dinner.

DUSTING FOR FINGERPRINTS

When others touch him they feel for clues in the tiny rills of his body,
          there,
a trespasser's mark remains before their own
my presence lies in invisible ink tracks along his spine,
                                                   waiting.

As he draws himself from her
she wonders if two bodies have separated or three
sensing the perfect fragment of another touch
resting in the curve of his arm
where she lies decoding the uneasy sense of pleasure,
refusing the temptation to ask
for fear of spoiling the present with the past,
he flinches
she detects
the similarity of skin brushing on skin,
personal etchings too deep to cover over
with new and shallow loves,
he makes the mistake, again
to think my touches were so soft
when they cut without drawing blood
a letter of passion and love forever tattooed to his heart,
there,
waiting,
when others touch him…

LEGAL

Now we smoke in bed
without spitting in ash trays in the dark
rolling butts in toilet paper and flushing.

Now we kiss on occasions
without getting off with each other
in telephone boxes down the precinct.

Now we have weekend breaks
without sneaking into your parents' bed
trying not to get pregnant.

Now we have dinner parties
without getting pissed till we throw up
over Debenham's shop front.

Now we stay in early
without going out late to nightclubs
daylight fucking our bones.

BAD SEX ON A SUNDAY

It seemed they ought to make the effort
after sitting in separate rooms for a week
bee-busy and important
but singular

a tired and short journey
forced on top
she felt her body fold in two
he didn't even bother
to watch her in the wardrobe mirror
just dried her up
quick swipe of dirty tea towel
(Ye Old Fighting Cocks
Exclusive to St Albans Tourist Centre),
then pulled out across a Sahara hallway
and left her masturbating over
Gregory Peck in the afternoon
on the old portable in the bedroom.

SINGULAR

'Awake, my St. John! leave all meaner things
To low ambition, and the pride of Kings.'
      (Alexander Pope, *An Essay on Man*)

You, Elgar's friend of a friend tend the dust of evenings,
play soft furnishings well, shuffling arm-rest covers. Ta da
hum! Dressed up as would-be magician in the decadence
of a towelling bathrobe, colours scattering. Abracadabra!
A plumped-up cushion for the neck, another for the arm
as the news at nine manifests itself onto a Pacific-wide,
surround-sound television screen. It seems you are always

planning a new and better trick, perhaps next winter a
part-time job after the best of a summer's tennis, but then
again not having to work could keep your mind busy for
a century. Living alone is a confidence trick when the bones
of a mother occupy the living/dining room with good china,
scatterings of doilies and a nest of awkward tables (mahogany
veneer), a taste you salute with an occasional Amontillado.

An inadequate frying pan makes it difficult to cook fried eggs
and nudges you closer to other decisions, modernisations of
the kind that take you from forty to fifty easily, when you
remember that getting married has been replaced by the
PowerMac 9600/350 in the box room/office and a complete
set of Shakespeare on CD-ROM. There between the lines
and your favourite bar stool other peoples' wives hide, all

sweetness and sling-back sandals, enough to get your blood
pumping, turning cold nights in a narrow bed to hot and
guilty delights. Before you turn over you watch those other
phantoms slink away, always too soon; the dream dates,
the real dates that ended, weather-forecasters, strangers you
noticed who did not notice you, cream-tea friends, the children
you never had, Sharon Stone, the smiling labrador who craps

on your car-parking space, the newsagent who might want to
kill you, Captain Ahab and other lost associations, leaving you
with an inexplicable draft wheezing through the newly-fitted
triple glazing and the remnants of 'Femme Fatale' in your
head (Side 2, Record 1, Andy Warhol's Velvet Underground
Featuring Nico, MGM Records, 1969). As eyes shut down and
darkness snuffs out each dim distraction, a chilling thought

remains, one into one is always one, their clothes will never
never hang in your wardrobe and squeeze-crease the Austin Reed
that waits now for important occasions or the bank manager to
invite him out. Shut up again, innards of a pyramid, but less
visited. Dust settling, forensic evidence, a cup and plate to wash
up, not enough rubbish to put out and an empty calendar of
old masters (free with Visa) hanging itself politely in the hall.

ABSENT

The last of a sky
takes the child
to the lip of
gentle waves
where a full
pleated tide winks,
the dance rinse
of her small feet
steals their beat
from the sand's
butterfly kiss
as the water rim
swallows her whole
and smooths
back the land
smiling gratefully.

IT IS DANGEROUS TO LEAN OUT OF THE WINDOW

This is not a holiday, they tell themselves, this is travel,
watching countries through train windows
and stray dogs in railway stations leaving and arriving.

Lookers-on see most of the game, but like a tapestry
their stitches aren't quite touching, struggling to
be part of the real places they are only ever visiting.

Broad minds are packed up small in rucksacks, and
Palaces and Duomos are ticked off with the same pen
that writes the postcards and notes the times of trains.

The Leaning Tower of Pisa is just pleased they came
if only for half an hour, it bends itself double
to make sure it can fit into the photograph.

The long night tickles them down tracks that will
never meet but end in equals signs at destinations
they burst into with an ever-tiring excitement.

Madrid cancels out Barcelona that cancels out Florence,
it is so hot, they bask in fountains in a park they find
out later, when leaving again, is called the Retiro.

Distant cousins of cities, those yellow rock stretches
outrun them, that old trick again when they thought
they were the ones moving but it was another train.

THE VANISHING POINT

It must have been a long time
since I saw your body so exposed,
usually you stayed home
beneath wise clothes,
now again giving birth from
your one piece to my two,
an uneasy equation evolves,
as we lie back, abroad and displaced,
you, old twists of driftwood, drying out,
lines cast by the batter of weathers.

Elongated I, no longer
cartwheeling across pre-pubescent sand,
now in perfect line with the sea
watching you from a bikini height,
all soft and not long caressed
spinning eyes as I skim by
towards a small shade
and you crease open your lids,
throw me
a jealous but proud gaze.

You are shrouded in your costume
no high cuts against your thighs
sensibly chosen from an
ocean-wide department store,
the waiters' young eyes search my flesh
flick rapidly across yours
and of course you care, don't care,
washed back briefly,
sexless debris up on the tide line
ignored by beachcombers.

You bruise easily,
have been bitten by mosquitoes
while I remain untouched and smooth,
but when we disappear
in the late-afternoon waves
somewhere we mingle bodies
and forget,
shedding skins in the warm water
where distorted limbs kick back
weightless and ageless.

CHAIR IN A MUSEUM

Do not touch or sit
arse full on once-
to-be-used chair,
now look with global
not-quite-round thoughts,
enjoy with the
bum crack of eyes,
make knees bend,
theory the weight
of this Frank Lloyd Wright 1955.
Set aside, Atlantic-swum
piece of art, not furniture
but elevated to a much higher seat
unhinged from dining table
and lesser known amputations
brothers and sisters
and farting dinner guests,
to be seen for its design
sat upon
only with good posture
and a stare
more museum than kitchen
well read and accepting,
that a chair is
not a chair is not a chair
when so well-travelled
and famous
legs more human than wooden,
more everlasting
than my own weak pins,
standing before it
on a Sunday
with nothing better to do
than learn to
appreciate a chair.

UNWRITTEN LAWS OF GALLERY

Visitors arrive into not a room but a Space, bored but looking interested in case someone is watching the picture features make by accident. Bodies walk and eyes see with a Pavlovian accuracy, quiet and slow, as if worried to upset the paintings or perhaps the attendant, suspended between looking part of the art or the other part which is not art. Tired or by review, people arranged on slim benches – dashes in sentences. Bumping up too close, a Hockney by a Munch, like rush hour, an armpit in your face, the desire to scream, but of course you don't, stay well inside the frame of what is known to be good behaviour. The exception, a stray who just came in to warm his bones, swears at Henry's holes, a quake of a noise to still the life, break a stride, long enough to let a brush stroke from Vincent's *Sunflowers* run out and

escape.

WAITING FOR A TOUCH

'Behold the sin for which I suffer, high
Enchained, with piercèd heart, beneath the sky.'
            (Aeschylus, *Prometheus Bound*)

I wear the clothes I bought
they stand on the curb asking for a spare fag
wearing the street that they found.

We still the traffic and the emptying theatres
Brian introduces himself by the tattoo
carved in a chain across his wrist below track lines.

Robbie talks fast clutching his sleeping bag
tells me the last hostel he stayed at
had syringes sticking up through the mattress.

We stand on the edge of that other London
where the lights and life are always bright
for those with the franchise for fire from the Gods.

Robbie makes me feel the quality of his coat
tells me he found it in a skip in Greek Street
wears it like it gave him golden wings.

I feel like a young mother
though we have only just met
worrying over nights turning cold and wet.

I give them a fiver and Robbie says 'Safe Man'
before they soak back into Soho
rolling away like a song someone else wrote.

THE SCAVENGER'S DAUGHTER

'The chief English sort of torture next after the rack is called the Scavenger's Daughter, in all respects the opposite of the rack, for while that drags apart the joints by the feet and hands tied, this, on the contrary, constricts and binds as into a ball. This holds the body in a three-fold manner, the lower legs pressed to the thighs, the thighs to the belly, and thus both are locked with two iron cramps which are pressed by the tormentor's force against each other into a circular form; the body of the victim is almost broken by this compression.'
(Matthew Tanner, seventeenth-century Jesuit writer)

and the sky connected to the world
and the world to the country
and the country to the city
and the city to your street
and your street to your house
and your house to your room
and your room to your body
and your body to the bruises
and the bruises to the pain
and the pain to the bruises
and the bruises to your body
and the body to your room
and your room to your house
and your house to your street
and your street to the city
and the city to the country
and the country to the world
and the world to the sky
and this weight only child
that you feel when the day dies done
is guilt
not from what you did wrong
but by never being right
which is why he says he didn't hit you
he just pushed you around a bit
for nothing more than breathing.

CASTINGS

He has the lips of a man I saw in Havana bending close to
kiss away the tears of his baby son on the Melicon, tender
and full, mango-wet, that could almost hurt you with their

attentions but fill you up with both longing and comfort,
making it all better. The fingers are mostly those of a busker
who lolls around Soho playing bad covers of Oasis, long, thin

trails that strum my hair and play smack me, but often he has
my father's hands when I can remember how they were,
old but good for holding suddenly on a cold Sunday walk

over the downs, a lick of warmth to fire the heart. His touch
is the simoom-dry man in the newsagent's who smells bad but
lets his hand linger just enough when he gives me my

change and it feels as if he has touched my whole body from
the inside out and I like it even though I find him disgusting.
The walk is always Richard Gere in *American Gigolo*, my

one famous concession (and the buttocks too if I get lazy
and want that ease of exposure). The voice, unfamous but
discovered, is Kevin something, Barclays cashier, who sounds

as he asks you how you want that, like he has chosen to tell
you the most beautiful secret in the world and I hold the two
twentys as close as a new baby, a momento echo. The eyes are

many distractions, a too-long stare back from a man glimpsed
on a Paris train, teasing black pools gone almost as soon as
they are seen, angry eyes that want to cry but hold a tear

balancing dangerously on their slim sills, the crinkled up
laughter eyes that dance and spit and spill such life they
drink you up with their swollen happiness, the thank-you

eyes from the fallen, the homeless, the insane when you
let yourself look back properly. A shoulder blade here, a way
of rolling a cigarette there, the surprise of finding the right

smile on a day I thought I was just doing the do. This is
the man I am making, in progress, whisper of action, take
one, always a fresh angle, never any complications. Then

the other man sneaks back in after so many dry months and
I see him as if for that first time, ten years ago, a clear sight,
stepping into a small sequin of sun in our lounge and my arms

pull him near without asking, want only him, familiar and
worn, and it hurts to love him so much in case he might not
be quite real or want to strip me of my best features and move on.

POPULATION COUNT

Less than a neighbour or a home-owner,
on streets adding up as pedestrian, drawn
to the accident that is always happening
close by, when saying and doing fall apart,
trying not to look and looking at another
pedestrian, now a body, shaking with the
fear of subtraction and never knowing
what their number was and where
exactly they came in the count, hoping
and fearing one in a million, at once
seen and then forgotten, covered over
by the next face and the next, passing...

DREAMS OF A WOMAN ASTRONAUT

Cassiopeia has the shape of either a W, an M, or a chair, depending
on how you look at it. When the famous nova of 1572 appeared,
this temporary or explosive star rapidly increased in magnitude
till it was as bright as Venus and could be seen in daylight. Within
two years it faded from view.

Padding out from the kitchen carrying tea,
stuck to slippers by a sudden and unwelcome thrust of gravity,
I saw you on the news in your Extravehicular Mobility Unit
floating with direction,
looking me straight in the eyes.

Your image Zeused my mortal bones,
you awakened my belief in goddesses with a lust for technology,
I changed your name to Cassiopeia, whispered it to the drafts,
wrote you imaginary letters and
launched them to a P O Box in space.

You were not attached to a heavy, private bodyland
but stepped on meteorites and spat in the face of planets,
you drew me up from formica plains to hitch a comet,
minds mixing with the infinite,
escaping from everyday galaxies.

I watched you flip, flounce, slide, all sommersaulting beauty,
as you listened to the secrets from the bellies of stars,
while the newspaper fools talked of the good job you had done,
tried to bring you back to earth,
wrote of domestic duties and sweat problems.

When you came back down I could not watch,
all that unzipping and interviewing and dragging at the sex of you
I kept the television switched off,
set to dream-making my own rocket
to blast through earthbound tragedy.

LEAVING THE BEACH

Arromanches Beach, Normandy, Summer

The sea runs itself out with flat waves,
retreats politely,
not unlike its counterpart of mill-pond postcard
sitting in smug piles
up on the promenade
beside molested nudes,
cartoon and otherwise.

Early evening empties the beach free
as the sun dips down,
unspectacular, perhaps tired,
while sand cascades from towels
and between toes
rocking up a small chaos
and a breeze in peacetime.

Walking back leisurely after hours on their backs
there is no need to start from the sound of a plane,
overhead,
white banner flails
advertising a hypermarket.

The ruins of the artificial port,
jutting out with a superficial covering of barnacles,
too young for fossils,
try to mix with the real old rocks,
seem at the time a good place to take a last photograph.

A child reluctantly leaves his sand boat behind,
tears blenching his eyes,
hanging back from the anchor of a parent arm.

People have written on the sand,
compelled to leave something behind,
mostly names that come and go,
words soon swallowed down by a deep swell,
perhaps a more suitable memorial
than those at Brouay or Cambes-en-Plaine
forced out of dry land to stand in neat rows,
while here a name lasts no longer
than the dark and tide
allow
and falls
where it lands.

ATTENDANTS

They make up for the lack of trees,
standing at points in a city,
a lift, a door, a department store,
perfecting one action,
pressing,
turning,
spraying,
depending on seasonal adjustments
and species. Double-take,
as if artificial, they might not seem
quite well, making bodies into
machines with a personal touch
and for the élite a few sentences,
real speaking, leaf mouths falling
a greeting at the mouth of a
restaurant, eyes made from a
disinterested make of glass
that can spook you out by
a look that feels like a
knife in the back.
Politeness hides the insides,
Russian dolls recurring, perhaps
tiny and invisible acts of genius,
composing,
painting,
debating,
are going on in parallel universes
and metaphysical doorways,
not still but moving, beyond our
own undoings which seem conscious
and independent, when all the time
we might be attendants, cloakroom
gals and boys who lost the tickets
and forgot why they were waiting.

RESTS IN THE MUSIC

Four Four. Common Time. Four crotchets or the same value in longer
or short notes or rests and four have to be counted in a bar.

1 2 3 4	This is it, mostly, before and after acts of doing,
2 2 3 4	waiting rooms, queues, nothing-special afternoons,
3 2 3 4	watching rain making out on windows,
4 2 3 4	playing patterns from curtains and shadows,
5 2 3 4	rolling a boggie in your fingers then eating it,
6 2 3 4	not the events that can be told properly,
7 2 3 4	when you ask me to tell you about my life,
8 2 3 4	but the uninteresting parts for those like me who aren't famous,
9 2 3 4	the jokes I can only half-remember or
10 2 3 4	the days-in doing nothing that sandwich days-out
11 2 3 4	the ones we focus upon that show a successful equation,
12 2 3 4	a point worth making about why I'm here
13 2 3 4	and what I've done that really matters.
14 2 3 4	Painful then when these are forgotten or grow hazy by the onslaught
15 2 3 4	of the just-being-here days, the rests in the music, hummings,
16 2 3 4	the passing of seconds, naked heartbeats,
17 2 3 4	failed by all words and all languages spoken or otherwise,
18 2 3 4	nightmares for biographers of any species.
19 2 3 4	I am often jolted awake by small details groping for attention,
20 2 3 4	dreams really are the worst filing cabinets, meticulously indexing,
21 2 3 4	this is where the grommets of life lie,
22 2 3 4	sneaking around in the dull rooms of a brain,
23 2 3 4	that extra space scientists are still trying to find,
24 2 3 4	but perhaps shouldn't bother about, because
25 2 3 4	it's there that these amoeba memoirs are,
26 2 3 4	taking the piss, lost neighbours and near strangers perhaps seen once
27 2 3 4	mixed up with the real friends and family you do see and can
28 2 3 4	string together in a well-constructed sentence of cause and effect.
29 2 3 4	Mostly, I'm just counting out the time after something happened
30 2 3 4	and before something else will happen again,
	like falling in love or nearly dying,
	those cymbal crashes we can talk about,

1 2 3 4   unlike the rest of it that leaves you there amongst the crowds
2 2 3 4   cloud watching and table tapping,
3 2 3 4   the tiny dots of life hanging about on the corners of insanity,
4 2 3 4   great gangs of futility beating up the little specks of real activity,
5 2 3 4   perhaps that's why some take to murder and smaller crimes,
6 2 3 4   just to get out from under the pressure of empty pages in diaries,
7 2 3 4   the dead-leg hours of being bored and aimless
8 2 3 4   that make talk of evolution and progress ridiculous,
9 2 3 4   when mostly, we're still playing monkeys,
10 2 3 4   picking scabs and foldings and washings and body functions,
11 2 3 4   visiting the toilet more often than other countries and
12 2 3 4   places we might have circled on maps
13 2 3 4   that try to interrupt this countdown to death.
14 2 3 4